THE BEAUTY WITHIN US

*An Anthology of
Inspirational Stories of Love,
Faith, and Triumph*

*Tenika Wilcox
Arlene Brathwaite
Raynika Wilcox
Shavina Richardson
Denise Harris
Martica Howard
Niroma Johnson
Kenneth Braswell
Inez Whitehead*

BRATHWAITE PUBLISHING
www.brathwaitepublishing.com

Brathwaite Publishing
P.O. Box 1202
Albany, New York 12201

ISBN – 10: 0692405666
ISBN – 13: 9780692405666

This book was printed in the United States of America.

For my three children: Raynika, Jalen, and Desmond
I love you with all my heart and soul.

ACKNOWLEDGMENTS

Thank you to Brathwaite Publishing for bringing my vision to fruition and to Arlene for giving of her time and gift to teach me about the art of writing and constructing a message. The people who inspired me are Denise Harris, Raynika Wilcox, Kenneth Braswell, Shavina Richardson, Niroma Johnson, Inez Whitehead, and Martica Howard. I offer special thanks to my sister, Camisha Pickens, for always being my sister friend. I thank my dad, Tenachie Pickens, for always speaking the truth. I thank my mom, Polly Pickens, and my brother Saul Jr. and Saul Sr. Roberts for composing a great support system.

INTRODUCTION

The vision for this book came to me in the grocery store. (I love to get in the longest line when checking out at the grocery store so that I can read the articles in the magazines without having to buy them. This is my way of saving money.) As I looked at the different covers for the articles that day, I saw *People* magazine's "50 Most Beautiful" issue. I started to ask myself, "What is beauty? How do you become one of the fifty chosen to represent beauty? Were they truly chosen for their beauty? What did they overcome? What did they do to give back to their community? What is it about them that makes them beautiful? Is it just the exterior?" These questions were the genesis of this book, and I have filled it with those who have inspired me and who have been inspired. These inspirational stories are of love, faith, and triumph. I feel that these three words are the real keys to the beauty within us that shines for all to see.

LOVE

BEAUTY WITHIN US
TENIKA WILCOX

I grew up a thin, brown-skinned girl with big eyes. I remember getting teased about how skinny I was and how big my eyes were. Throughout my childhood I was reminded of my insecurities and told repeatedly what I would or would not be. I remember growing up where beauty always defined how you were treated: if you were light skinned and had nice hair, you were treated better. If you were a shade darker, you were treated as a second-class citizen.

School Daze (a movie that touched on issues related to skin tone and hair texture) reminds me of the issues that were real in our family. Family members were treated better and were told how successful they would be because they were pretty. This love was shown only for these family members, and at times I was left to reflect on how inadequate I was compared to them. These inadequacies all came in areas of how I looked. This issue often left me with low self-esteem about how I looked and how I related to others. I thought, *Why me?*

I honestly don't know where my drive to succeed and prove people wrong about their false statements about me came from. I think it had to do with proving that I mattered and that others *would* recognize me and what I could bring to this world. I see this same drive to succeed in my daughter—she wants to prove all the naysayers wrong. I believe that I can do whatever I put my mind to despite a lack of support from those family members who tried to keep me down and keep me in that downward cycle. What I know now is that I may not be the prettiest on the outside, but I find that it takes more than looks to get where you need to go and what you want to be in life. Beauty is within us all and reflects out.

Tenika Wilcox is an elementary school teacher in Troy, New York. Her academic accomplishments include earning a master of science in education and reading and a bachelor of science in elementary education and sociology from Sage College and an associate's degree in elementary education preparations.

Tenika has been teaching for nineteen years. She was selected as the Capital Regions Educator of the Week. She was a candidate for New York Teacher of the Year. Tenika developed a character education curriculum that implemented an after-school reading and tutoring program for the city of Troy.

Tenika founded United Sisters of New York Inc. in 2003. The organization is dedicated to supporting personal growth among women and supporting women's education by providing scholarships to women who want to pursue their educational goals.

Tenika is president of her Kiwanis chapter of Troy, New York; an alumnus of the YMCA Black and Latino Achievers Program; assistant manager of Her Temple Monologues; and a member of a number of other groups and organizations through which she supports the community.

MY DAD MY HERO
MARTICA HOWARD

Inspiration—what is it, who is it, and how does it come about? Is it magical or inherited? Can one borrow it or purchase it? Is one allowed to have more than the next person? Intriguing, right? Exactly my point.

Looking over my life, I've come to the conclusion that I was born of inspiration—the inspiration of my ancestors who worked tirelessly to provide for their families. The inspiration of their countless hours manning the farmland and crops, picking cotton, maneuvering plywood trucks, and oftentimes lacking food or money to survive. My father often told me stories about growing up in a rural part of Alabama

(Choctaw County) with five siblings, a stay-at-home mother, and a father who worked daily to support the family. "Impoverished but happy" was the theme I gathered from the many stories he told me, ending our conversations in chuckles while wearing a smile. They had few materialistic items, but they were a family full of love and togetherness. Dad challenges me often with thoughts of how the world has abundant resources but less appreciation of our brethren. He would often share this story, which has now become a staple in my memory. He told me, "You know that growing up we had one bike among us children, and we shared that bike and took care of that bike." He ended the story by saying, "I guess things are just different now."

Looking back on my life of thirty-seven years, I must admit to being self-centered and at times taking a minimalist approach to tasks while expecting favorable results. It was not until I reached true maturation through having my own child, personal struggles, and maintaining my own household that I was able to appreciate the long, drawn-out conversations with my father. He'd often begin by taking a deep breath before diving in, discussing the approach he'd take with me when I wasn't being honest or fulfilling my potential. I'd shrug, roll my eyes, and respond in a bored tone. "Yes, Dad, I already know." But what did I really know? It was not until later in life that I realized he was one of very few people who had my best interests at heart: always encouraging me, picking me up when I was down, or knowing something was wrong without my saying a word. Our connection is unexplainable at times. People often let me down in life, but he is one person who hasn't failed me yet.

Many things stand out when I think of my father. Perhaps this is the most inspirational story. It's a story of ethics, hard work, determination, struggle, and perseverance. I think I was about fourteen or fifteen years old when I learned how and why my father worked so hard for our family. As my brother prepared for his senior year of high school and many college visits, my father changed his shift at work (Watervliet Arsenal) from a day shift to a night shift, which allowed him to obtain a day job in construction and continue his education in the evening at Hudson Valley Community College. So let's imagine this: an 11:00 p.m. to 7:00 a.m. shift, a 7:30 a.m. to 2:00 p.m. shift, and then college from 5:00 p.m. to 8:00 p.m. Are you exhausted? Well, I am from just the thought of working around the clock. He always said, "You just do what you have to do, and keep going." I never asked Daddy why; I just knew it was for extra money to send my brother to college. My father worked several days a week, never complaining, and still keeping our home in order while graduating from college himself during that time. He continued at this workload for an extended period to ensure a quality education for my brother and him. During this time he stopped smoking cigarettes (cold turkey) and eagerly engaged in more physical activity. I can remember saying, "Dad, I'm having a bad day." His response was—and still is—"You don't know what a bad day is." How right he was. However, what I do know is that he inspires me every day to work and give my best effort and to be kind, smile a little, and do my very best. For you never know when you may need someone.

I have been abundantly blessed in this lifetime to have a person that inspires me, pushes me, and demands more of me than I sometimes do of myself. Thanks, Dad, for laying the groundwork for me to have a better life. He did the work, and with every task, there was a teachable moment for me to see how to do things a better way and learn from my mistakes. My father dreamed and achieved, and if I'm lucky enough in this life, I will manage to lay the same groundwork for my son.

Martica Howard was born and raised in Albany, New York. While in elementary school, she had a love for writing and always thought about a career as a journalist. As she matured, goals changed and she ultimately did not pursue that path. Instead, she majored in Community & Human Services for her undergraduate studies at the State University of New York pursing her passion to help others.

A few years later a colleague suggested that she attend graduate school and get a Master's Degree. It all started with one class she thoroughly enjoyed and within eighteen months she had obtained a Master's degree in Administration of Criminal Justice while raising a young son, and working full-time with inmates throughout various prisons in New York State.

THE TEST OF TIME
ARLENE BRATHWAITE

"Arlene, are you busy this weekend?" my friend Yvonne asked.

"No, why?"

"I need someone to ride with me to the prison to visit my husband."

"Okay," I responded hesitantly.

"Great."

Great? There's nothing great about going to prison. She had no idea how bad I wanted to say "Hell no," but I didn't want her to think I thought any less of her because she was doing time with her man. I never understood why a beautiful woman with such a good job and close-knit family would stay in a relationship with a man who had nothing to offer her rather than move on and find a man who could take care of her the way a woman is supposed to be taken care of. Over the years, I watched in utter bewilderment as Yvonne and women like her got on the road every weekend, sometimes driving six to eight hours one way, just to sit in a prison visiting room with their husbands or boyfriends. *I will* never *do that*, I thought.

But there I was, five years later, on my way to a correctional facility to visit my husband. I remember the days before my husband went to prison. The words "I love you" would roll off our tongues as easy as telling each other "Good morning," or "Have a nice day at work." This is why I believe prison became the ultimate test for our love. Could our love really stand the test of time—literally?

Our first test came when he was arrested and sentenced to fifteen years to life. Before I could fully process what was happening, he was in a maximum-security prison way up in the mountains on the border of Canada.

I immediately thought of all the women I knew who were visiting loved ones in facilities, and I finally understood why they did it. When you truly love someone, you cannot—you will not—abandon that person.

My second test came when I had to visit my husband at South Port Correctional Facility. South

Port is a special housing unit for New York State's most violent criminals. My husband is far from violent, but he got caught up in a riot and wound up in there for two years. All I did on the drive up was pray. Pray that my husband was all right, pray that my car would make it there and back, and pray that I wouldn't wind up in some kind of accident in these mountains.

You see, the mountains are very cold and lonely—not only because of the weather but also because of the people. Most people never stop on their travel there because of the prejudices the mountains hold. I never stopped unless it was absolutely necessary.

Once I arrived at the facility, nothing could've prepared me for what lay ahead of me. Once I was processed, I entered the visiting room. It reminded me of a dog kennel. It had cages within cages. The cages were painted a dull yellow, almost beige. People's voices were so loud that they were vibrating off of the steel walls.

As I slowly walked in to find the cage with my husband's number on it, I watched people laughing and talking as if this were normal. Once I made it to the side where my visit was to take place, there were vending machines where I could purchase something to eat while on the visit.

I decided that I would accept my situation for what it was and enjoy this so-called visit because I knew if my husband sensed in any way that this situation was too much for me, it would only make his stay worse. He could deal with whatever punishment they sent his way, but he could never handle watching me hurt. That in itself would make it difficult for him to do his time.

I purchased a few items from the vending machines—particularly a cup of soda. I found it hard to believe that they actually had a fountain machine in the visiting room because in most facilities, you find the typical vending machines, the ones that have cans or plastic bottles. In any case, I purchased a cup of soda for my husband to have with his food.

I proceeded to my seat, and as I waited patiently for my husband to come down, I noticed that the cages were smeared with lipstick and the bars had a nauseating stench to them. I thought to myself, *I would never place my lips near these bars. How disgusting would that be? All the germs and only God knows what else on them.*

After waiting about an hour for my husband to come down for the visit, I watched in horror as he was instructed to walk out of the entrance door backward. He wore body and ankle shackles and handcuffs. His hair was long and unruly. As he sat, I noticed that his chair was chained to the floor. The guard left without removing the shackles.

"Is he going to take those off?" I asked my husband.

"No, these have to stay on for the whole visit. In here, I'm not different from the mass murderers or serial rapists. In here, we're all the same. One big dysfunctional family," he said with a smile to try and lighten the mood. But I could see the pain in his eyes. My soul cried out to hold him close—to drain away his pain and carry it out of there with me.

We talked for a while, and he reassured me that he wouldn't be there long, that his case would be reversed. Once he calmed me down long enough to stop crying and listen, we decided that any burden God placed on us, together we could see it through.

When our visit came to an end, I closed my eyes, held my breath, and kissed my husband good-bye through the same bars that I said I would never touch. And that's when I realized that the women who came before me probably said exactly what I first said when I first entered the visiting room. This situation was one of the many difficult memories of being a prisoner's wife.

The test of our love took us to hell and back. Yes, my husband is home now. So many of the little things we took for granted before he went to prison we now cherish. Prison was the lowest part of our lives; we both still have nightmares, and as crazy as it might seem, the trials and tribulations of prison not only challenged my beliefs, but they also changed them. Love, to me, is no longer just a four-letter word. Love is an overwhelming, breathtaking, soul-touching experience. So know that if you've experienced love, you have been blessed with a gift that has eluded many and has only been bestowed on a few.

Arlene Brathwaite is an author who was born and raised in Albany, New York, and is the founder and co-owner of Brathwaite Publishing. She attended Sage College, where she majored in computer science. In 2006, She propelled herself into the literary world with her debut novel, *Youngin'*. Her status as an author not to be taken lightly was cemented with the follow-up, *Ol' Timer*. In a span of five years, Arlene wrote and published five more novels (*In the Cut, Paper Trail, Soul Dancing, Darkest before Dawn*, and *Casualties of War*). Through Brathwaite Publishing, her novel *Darkest before Dawn* has been made into a feature film, and her novel *In the Cut* is now a web series.

FAITH

CANCER KICKIN'
INEZ WHITEHEAD

When I was diagnosed with stage IIIB breast cancer in 2001, I was frozen in time. At that time, the only thing I knew about any cancer was that if you have it, you die. I agonized over things, wondering, *Am I going to dwindle away and die a painful death? How do I tell my kids? Do I have enough time to get things in order? Who will take care of my husband?* My mind went on and on. I looked for someone to talk to who had been diagnosed with my stage of cancer. When I couldn't find any, I thought the worst. I was told that once people go through their ordeals with cancer, they don't want to talk about them. I got on my knees and promised God that if he got me through this, I would become that voice. Well, he upheld his end of the bargain, and I'm keeping mine. My new life began after cancer.

I wrote my book, *Cancer Kickin' Warrior*: it's the ultimate feel-good cancer-survivor book. The stories in this book are not just about me; they are about people who have fought and won their battles with every type and stage of cancer. Like me, the people in this book wanted to share their stories to let anyone going through this know that it is not a death sentence.

I also write a column called Cancer Kickin' Warrior for two newspapers in upstate New York. In it I tell stories like the ones in my book and give information regarding the newest treatments, medicines, and clinical trials that are available. I engage in motivational speaking and counsel people who are going through a rough time with cancer. In addition, I serve on the board of the Women's League Cancer Patient Aid in Greene County, New York. People often ask me why it is I don't get paid for everything I do. My answer is simple: "God paid me thirteen years ago when my life was saved, so now I owe him!"

My motto to anyone who has suffered the trials and tribulations of cancer is this: "What is the point of surviving if you're not going to live?" Help someone else become a cancer-kickin' warrior!

Inez Whitehead is a nine-year stage IIIB breast cancer–kickin' warrior. Aside from her numerous charitable works, she writes a column called Cancer Kickin' Warrior in the Catskills. She attended John Jay College of Criminal Justice in New York. She received her AS degree from Essex County College in New Jersey and her BS from Thomas Edison State College in New Jersey. She enjoys spending time with her husband, Mike; her beloved grandchildren; and her dogs.

WHEN REVELATION STIRS INSPIRATION
KENNETH BRASWELL

When you seek inspiration, one of the hardest things to do is determine which is the most significant of all the people, things, and events that inspire you. I struggled writing this piece because so many things have inspired me at different times and moments in my life. Some of my greatest inspirations have come from situations and events that caused me some level of pain—particularly incidences of loss, such as the death of a family member, the end of a business, the loss of a job, or the ending of a relationship.

Pain certainly has a way of inspiring us in ways that are not so beneficial, such as imploding into self-pity, embarrassment, or depression. It can also lead us to seek revenge and retribution. Ironically, the most painful moments of my life have produced the biggest and most positive elements of my life.

Then there are those things in life that bring us joy. All of my children have inspired some measure of positive change in my life. From my oldest, Tiarrah, I learned that being young and imprudent is not an excuse for not taking care of your responsibilities. Amber has impressed upon me that just because a child is not biologically mine, I could still have a fatherly impact in her life. Nzinga continues to remind me that at some point in life, you have to grow up and be responsible, while KJ continues to teach me that a son is a precious blessing and a true reflection of how I see myself. In addition to my children, the stability of my marriage to a wonderful woman who clearly understands and supports my passions and purpose; the cooperative, co-parental relationships with the mothers of my children; and the spiritual grounding in a church that provides me the space to worship, learn, be supported, and develop my relationship with God all bring incredible amounts of joy to my life. And of course, there is the amazing inspiration derived from seeing the impacts of my professional work with fathers and families.

As you can see, it becomes quite difficult to identify one inspirational person or event when you are immersed in inspiration all the time. Therefore, if I were to say what or who inspires me, the answer would have to be inspiration itself. I am addicted to being inspired. I look for it in everything that I do, every conversation I have, and every person and experience with which I engage. It is like following breadcrumbs or the yellow brick road. I believe the most fulfilling part of obtaining goals and accomplishments is the journey itself, in which the beginning and end are just props in the story line of life.

Recently, on a trip from Malaysia, I had the chance to watch *Jobs*—the life story of Steve Jobs, former CEO of Apple. I had heard about Steve and knew that there was something unique about him, which is what made me curious to watch the movie. I had no idea that I would cry through most of the documentary and that it would keep me paralyzed for the rest of the flight home, and for days after. What struck me about Steve Jobs is what people misunderstood about him—the same misunderstanding I believe people have about me: How can one man have the outrageous notion that he can change the world? Steve believed he could change the world by creating a product that would change human behavior and become an extension of one's self. For me, changing the world means restoring the passion of fatherhood for the purpose of deeply loving our children so much that being without them would be equivalent to being without air itself. Ron Williams, a close and respected friend, once said to me, "I don't understand how people call themselves living when they don't have something in life to which they can't breath without." It is not a farfetched concept once you understand that inspiration is what happens when passion and purpose come together.

Jobs climaxed for me when I looked down and realized that while I was watching the movie, my iPhone was sitting on my knee. At that moment, I understood. I realized that passion is just nervous energy without purpose. I also realized at that moment that *inspiration* is a verb—that purpose and passion can inspire (move) you to clutch the things you believe—good or bad. I believe Steve Jobs had this inspiration for Apple, Dr. King had it for equality, Malcolm X had it for the injustices faced by black people, I have it for fatherhood, and Jesus had (and has) it for salvation.

The movie closed with Steve Jobs saying, "People thought I was crazy for wanting to save the world, when in fact you have to be to want to do so." I don't completely agree with that statement; that is, crazy can help, but you must be inspired beyond anyone else's understanding or desires to support or agree with your purpose to make a change in the world.

Passion and purpose will ultimately determine your position. At times people will look at your title, education, lifestyle, upbringing, economic status, religion, or age and wonder why you are where you are or why you do what you do. Here's what *inspiration* wants you to understand: passion and purpose will place you in positions that credentials and humankind alone do not have the ability to create or to take away.

Be inspired!

Kenneth Braswell (www.fathersincorporated.com) is the executive director of Fathers Incorporated, a nonprofit organization that serves as a leader in the promotion of responsible fatherhood and mentoring. Since 2004, the agency's main focus has been on the development of support and services for fathers.

As a national motivational speaker, presenter, and trainer, Braswell addresses both youth and adults, motivating them to be hopeful about life. He also authored *When the Tear Won't Fall* and a workbook, *Gentle Warriors*. Additionally, Braswell hosts *Dad's Eye View*, a Time Warner Cable access television program aimed at parenting from a father's perspective. As a result of his life's experience, Braswell has been featured or mentioned in such publications as *Essence, The Crisis, Gospel Today, Capital Region Parent Pages*; BSI International's *In Search of Fatherhood®*;

the *Philadelphia Inquirer,* the *Times Union,* and various other media forums.

In 2010, Fathers Incorporated launched a cause marketing campaign entitled "Ties Never Broken," whose mission is to highlight responsible fatherhood and mentoring. Inspired by President Obama, the campaign is designed to increase the efforts of serving and supporting responsible fathers. The campaign uses the icon of a blue bow tie (a lapel pin) as the symbol of responsible men.

Born and raised in Brooklyn, Mr. Braswell is the father of four beautiful children, an uncle, a grandfather, and the husband to his beautiful wife, Tracy.

THE LOST CHILD WITHIN NIROMA JOHNSON

I did not like myself growing up. I experienced moles-tation at the age of six by a teenage girl who lived not far from my grandmother's house. I was too afraid to tell anyone and kept it to myself. I felt that if my mother found out, she might kill this girl. When I was nine, I had to start changing. diapers, and I was forced to deal with adult responsibilities. I had resentments and could not let go of it for many years. When I was old enough to stay out, I did just that. It was like I was a runaway child, running wild. I had so much anger inside me that I was not aware of it until I was much older. I also had a lot of self-hatred within me. I did not like myself and thought I was the ugly duckling.

I started to mess with boys, looking for love in all the wrong places, and was raped at the age of fifteen by a boy I liked. My mother gave me a choice of having the child or not, and I chose not to because I was young and afraid. I became a follower at the age of twelve and smoked a cigarette like my friends did. When I was sixteen, going on seventeen, I smoked weed like my associates. I then decided to do drugs, and this took me down a long road where there was no light to see my way out. It was God's grace and mercy that saved me from the horrors of addiction. I also experienced verbal and physical abuse for many years, and today I will not allow anyone to beat on me without me doing something about it.

The motivating fact in my life was God letting me know that he would take me out of here if did not stop. I realized that I did not have the right to take my own life. I wanted to see my grandchildren grow up, so this stayed in my head. I am a much better person today. I thank God for His favor on me. These are words of encouragement: "No cross, no crown. No pain, no gain. Faith and Fear cannot occupy the same space. Don't give up, no matter what. You are special and a child of God. God has your back!" These are all slogans that people would say to me throughout my life.

I had to take on responsibilities of an adult because my mother had to work and could not pay a babysitter. I felt like the ugly duckling because I could not see my true beauty within, and I felt like the unwanted child. I felt I was being punished. I used to rebel as a young child because I rarely got to play due to my responsibilities on top of doing homework.

I used to read my grandfather's Bible at the age of five, but when I got older, I realized that God was reading to me. I was too young to read the Bible, yet I was always in the book. What inspires me today is when other people who have experienced trials and tribulations still press on. Life is full of ups and downs, but we have to push on with God leading the way.

Niroma Johnson, a comedienne, poet, and actress, was born and raised in Brooklyn, New York. She grew up being a class clown with both family and friends, but she never thought about doing comedy until later in life because she was very shy. She started doing comedy for the N/A Fellowship for fund-raising events and at conventions.

Niroma went to the Apollo back in October of 2010. She was nervous and could not get through ninety seconds onstage for the audition. She later decided that she needed to go to open mics so that she could become comfortable on stage. Niroma has been comfortable onstage since then. She also loves acting and was in a feature film called *Dirty Little Secrets* that was produced by Brathwaite Publishing (2014).

.

TRIUMPH

MY GREATEST CHALLENGE
RAYNIKA WILCOX

The greatest challenge that I overcame was having a learning disability. To have a learning disability has its ups and downs, but with perseverance and a strong support system, I was able to rise above the stigma that comes with having a learning disability.

Harriet Tubman once said, "Every great dream begins with a dreamer. Always remember you have within you the strength, the patience, and the passion to reach for the stars to change the world." I like this quote because it defines the way I live my life. I compare myself to Harriet Tubman because she paved the way to freedom, and I am paving the way to help people with the challenges of having a learning disability. During my fifth grade year, I was struggling with comprehension in class, and I was giving it all I had, but I still couldn't get the concept of it. I remember getting frustrated and depressed because I couldn't get to the same level as my classmates in a rigorous academic program. My resource teacher realized that I had a learning disability: Central Auditory Processing Disorder. My resource teacher thought that maybe wearing an earpiece in class could solve these problems. When I first got my earpiece, I was nervous to use it in class—of incurring the stigma of *appearing* to have a disability on top of *actually* having one.

I realized after using the earpiece for a while and with the encouragement of my family and friends that the device helped with my educational deficits, and I started to slowly progress in my classes and get better grades. I learned many lessons in life, and one of them was that no matter how many accomplishments you have (and in spite of the struggles you have gone through in life to achieve those accomplishments), there will always be negative people who try to lower your self-esteem and plant doubts about your ability to succeed.

I am sad to say that some of those people were my own teachers in school. They would tell me that I couldn't do this or that or take this class and that my dream to become a pediatrician would be too hard due to my disability. The counselor scoffed at me when I told him I wanted to apply to this college. My counselor's response was that I would never get in. The more I heard this criticism, the more I doubted my ability to do as many things as other students could do. It took me a long time to get past those challenges of having a disability and to take the time to realize that if I want to go for something, I'm going to go for it because it's my life and it's my choice. In spite of my disability, I was selected as one of the 2010 members of the Halfmoon Voyage and received the 2010 President Education Award from President Obama. I am currently president of Rensselaer High School Key Club and president of Jr. United Sisters of NY Inc. I was vice president of the Rensselaer High School Key Club; a member of the Rensselaer High School Student Council; the 2013 alumnus for Empire Girls State; a finalist for Girls Nation; and a runner-up for the 2014 Rensselaer County Miss Uncle Sam. I currently hold the Rensselaer High School four-hundred-meter dash record, and I was the 2013 MVP for track and field.

I work hard and continue to persevere despite my disability and would be a valuable asset to any college I attend. The award I receive from this scholarship would help me to achieve the goal I have set for myself of becoming a pediatrician. I strive to remain a voice to show people that you should never let anything or anyone stop you from what you want to do, and if you just believe in yourself and keep moving forward, you can get anywhere in this world.

RESILIENCE IN THE MIDST OF THE STORM
SHAVINA RICHARDSON

I n November 2005, I was confronted with the reality that my husband, the man who took a vow before God to love me "for better or for worse," was cheating. His adultery weighed on my heart and defined the pure essence of rage. The anger that came through my chest was undefined but noted as the very factor of disruption. He took a chance on another and destroyed our family. There was no going back because prior to his disrespectful act, I'd seen the signs, but I'd wanted to save the marriage. I wanted so badly not to become a statistic. I wanted so badly to be more than the sum of my parts. I wanted us. The man that I had known since the tender age of fourteen—I wanted my family.

As I read the e-mails describing their involvement—I wanted to reach out and touch someone. However, that wasn't an option. Instead, I confronted the man who betrayed me. I confronted my soul mate—I confronted my husband. His reaction was one of pure shock, but his inflated chest had him believing that he was justified because he was the primary caretaker; he was the one "bringing home the dough." He was the one making things happen, and I was "just a housewife." I'll never forget him telling me that he "didn't need to rush home to me." Those words hurt me to the core, but I let him rest in it as I grabbed his phone and broke it in half in rage. He left and vowed never to return. He vowed that I would come running back—because "no one will ever be as good to you as I have…No one will ever love you the way I have…*You need me!*"

Those words gave me the strength never to look back. ("Never" was a word I had been conditioned "never" to say.) I then made my own vow—to finish college, to honor my father in heaven, to take care of my kids, not to return home to my mother's house, to work hard enough to do better than *he* ever thought I could, and to be better than all the *I can't believers*, all the *I told you Sos*, and all the *haters*.

So after all the court battles, after all the restraining orders, I was granted full, sole, and legal custody of our children. Two years later, a divorce provided me with the freedom to begin again. Yes, I changed the way I viewed men, changed the way I viewed my life. In that moment, I claimed victory over trials and gave it all to God. In that moment I chose me and mine—yes, I regained my life. I regained *me*!

Shavina Renee Richardson, a.k.a. Bklyn Shay, is the product of Crown Heights, Brooklyn, New York. Upstate became her home in September 2001. Shavina has been performing, writing, singing, drawing, and painting since the tender age of eight. In 2008, she became more active in the art of the spoken word. Developing a true passion for communication and the arts, she turned more to the production side of it. Obtaining her master of social work from the University at Albany is one of her vast accomplishments, but the greatest is her role as a mother of three beautiful kids. Shavina is a member of United Sisters of New York Inc. and an active participant in local community advocacy groups. Shavina currently resides in Albany, New York. Shavina's latest project is *Her Temple Monologues*, a spinoff of *The Vagina Monologues*. Written by playwright and activist Eve Ensler and based on dozens of interviews Ensler conducted with women, the play addresses women's sexuality and the social stigma surrounding rape and abuse, creating a new conversation about and with women. *Her Temple Monologues* invites you to a world of courage, love, hope, strength, passion, and the will to live in the midst of the storm. We also encourage you to think outside the box, listen with an open heart, and embrace your power.

FINDING MY PURPOSE
DENISE HARRIS

If you bungle raising your children,
I don't think whatever else you do
matters very much.

—JACKIE KENNEDY

I was a lost child from the moment of my birth in 1964. My mother died during childbirth. Against medical advice that she would possibly not make it—for she had only one kidney—she chose to give birth to me anyway. I will never know why she made that decision. I have many theories, but only God knows the real reason. Although I do not recall my infancy,

I have memories from being two years old. They are as clear as if they were happening today. All of my childhood, I never knew why I was here or where I belonged. I recall feeling sad and lost, which made me angry. Honestly, I felt like an animal. I was always fighting with my nephews Calvin and Corey—mainly Calvin, because Corey was sweet. They were the ones I made most of the childhood memories with: school, dinner, and the importance of sticking together. However, I formed a bond with my niece Tenika that has survived throughout the years. I tear up just thinking about it. I kidnapped her once from day care when she was just approximately four years old. I remember going in and telling them that my brother had sent me in to pick her up, and they believed me, and we proceeded to take the bus to Tops department store, where I shoplifted her a black doll (I was a militant even at eight). Then we took another bus to the playground, where we were caught by my sister, who spotted us. I think about it now—you can't make this stuff up. Over forty years later, we talk almost daily. Tenika made me happy during those very dark days and still does to this day.

With my appointed godmother to my brother, Albert, and his wife, Polly (Tenika's parents), and my sister, Ruby, I was never happy. But I have always looked up to Ruby because she was always strong and successful, and she was my inspiration. I spent a lifetime feeling I was an obligation, burden, or disappointment to many. Looking back, I now know this led to a path of destruction, starting with my being molested by my godmother's nephew and my sister-in-law's two brothers, which led to my promiscuous behavior. A vivid memory is of being molested by one brother: the younger brother walked in on us, and I just lay there. I knew it was wrong, but I was helpless. I probably was about five to seven years old, but I know now that I was too young to have a grown man on top of me and penetrating me. I have heard professional psychiatrists say that children have no memory, and I wish that were true, but I do have vivid memories—almost as if it happened only an hour ago—because it was a part of my life until I was sixteen years old. Now I know why I was so angry all the time. Maybe if I had said something, I could have changed the course of my life, but I didn't until I was married. Everything is so clear now: why I never did well academically until the eleventh grade and why I became promiscuous. I lacked knowledge about sexual activity and was ignorant at seventeen about bringing a child into this world.

Another truth is that I had an abortion when I was fifteen after becoming pregnant by a boyfriend. Never for an instant did I think of the consequences of having a baby. Nowadays there are organizations and classes that educate you. Even if they only reach a few, maybe I could have been one of them. I turned eighteen in November and had a daughter in January 1983. Fresh out of high school, I knew her life would be different from mine. When I was pregnant, I knew I would protect my child with my life, and I did just that with my daughter Lavonia. She changed my life forever because I then had a purpose, and I never looked back. Everybody counted me out and thought I would be a welfare mom and amount to nothing, just becoming another statistic. Despite all the odds stacked against me, I made it.

Becoming a mother was one thing I can say I not only was good at but excelled at. I would go through fire to make sure my children had a different path to success than I did, and I knew college would be their ticket. I knew with education they would not have to struggle, tolerate, or settle like I had. Now I have my own ticket to punch; I never envisioned myself pursing college because I thought I was stupid—just not college material. However, after a long, successful career, I had become complacent, as if I were chained to that career because I was not intelligent enough to do anything else. I realized that I had envisioned and orchestrated the path for my daughter to be successful, for I knew that from my working at the Hotel Thayer at West Point for nine years that Lavonia would attend West Point. I remember watching those parents come through the hotel on graduation day so proud, and I knew this was the best institution for her to attend. However, I knew nothing about the admission process or how strenuous it would be. I only knew that she would attend. Never once did it enter my mind that being African American would have an impact. I thought a black female would be elite. In May 2007, Lavonia became a West Point graduate, and in 2009, my husband, Dornn became a University of Notre Dame graduate. I knew I could attend college as well because I thought that was brilliant. Unexpectedly, I walked away from a twenty-six-year career to further my education in accounting.

Although I was afraid, it was something I had to do for me. I knew that the world was evolving at a rapid pace, enlarging the hole in my existence. I continually asked myself, *Who am I? What is my purpose?* My purpose in life could not just to be to raise children, even if I felt vindicated against the nonbelievers. I'm now facing my fears; I'm competing and winning. My life now is just beginning, and I'm running my own race while preparing for a marathon because the sky is the limit. However, I still have to at times give myself a little pep talk: that I *can* and I *will*. Finally, I no longer live *through* or *for* my children—I'm living for me. For I now know that "my biggest accomplishment is to save me, so I can see the success of my daughters and break the cycle."

Denise Michelle Harris was born to Robert Lee and Dora Pickens on November 12, 1964. Denise lost her mother at birth, and without the guidance of her mother, she looked for inspiration and mentorship in her sister, Ruby, and niece and best friend, Tenika. By her senior year, Denise had given birth to her daughter, Lavonia, on January 1, 1983, a blessing in disguise. Denise would defy the stereotypes of a teen mother by graduating from high school and providing the best life possible for her child. She joined the US Navy. By the age of twenty-two, Denise was married to her current husband of twenty-nine years, Dornn Harris.

Denise was a strict mother who instilled discipline, hard work, and respect into her daughters. Her expectations were clear: keep your head in your books if you want to be somebody. Denise knew that for her daughters to be successful, she had to be their example. After twenty-six years in the hospitality business, she resigned from her job and enrolled in college in 2013. In May 2015, Denise will receive her degree in accounting. Like her children, she too maintains an A average. She is a member of the Phi Theta Kappa Honor Society. Upon graduation, she plans to open her own accounting business. Denise's main message to her daughters and all women is that it is never too late to achieve your dream.